TESTIMONIALS

"This is a terrific publication presenting historical background, insight into the editions, setup options, part assignments, and practical performance suggestions for The Rite of Spring. Percussionists will find this very useful in approaching Stravinsky's masterpiece."

- Raynor Carroll
Principal Percussion, Los Angeles Philharmonic, Retired

"Chris delves deep into the inner workings of what is arguably the most iconic piece in the repertoire. With so many editions, changes, and interpretations available, Chris does a fantastic job of offering context and helpful past performance practices, while still leaving room for your own ideas. Furthermore, the historical background and information he provides sheds light into Stravinsky's compositional process, which is an invaluable tool for anyone who performs this piece. This is a must read for all percussionists. BRAVO, Chris!"

-Jauvon Gilliam
Principal Timpanist, National Symphony Orchestra

"It is fun to read and brings up some great points which give us some interesting things to think about, and strive for, when performing this great work."

-Jeffrey Fischer
Principal Timpanist, Boston Ballet and Boston Lyric Opera Orchestras

"This is an essential contribution. Stravinsky's scores are notoriously treacherous for percussionists (see: L'Histoire du soldat). In this work, Chris is able to create an engaging and personal map for any percussionist to succeed in a performance of another behemoth: *The Rite of Spring*. For a conductor, this type of knowledge is essential as throughout the work, performers will rely on the conductor's sound preferences for choice of equipment and execution. Chris details the essential places where this will be sure to happen and I now feel better prepared to conduct this work and vitally aware of the host of options available to me as an interpreter."

-John Devlin
Music Director, Wheeling Symphony Orchestra

"Written in a clear and concise style, this is an invaluable addition to scholarship devoted to Stravinsky's Rite of Spring. Chris DeChiara has provided an outstanding roadmap to one of the towering masterpieces of the 20th century. The Rite of Spring, A Percussionist's Guide, is essential reading for conductors and percussionists preparing this complex masterpiece."

-Emil de Cou, Music Director, Pacific Northwest Ballet; Conductor, National Symphony Orchestra at Wolf Trap

THE RITE OF SPRING

A PERCUSSIONIST'S GUIDE

CHRIS DECHIARA

Copyright © 2020 by Chris DeChiara

All rights reserved.

No part of this book may be reproduced in any form or by any electronic or mechanical means, including information storage and retrieval systems, without written permission from the author, except for the use of brief quotations in a book review.

Cover concept by Chris DeChiara

Cover design by Hristo Kovatliev

CONTENTS

Preface	ix
Introduction	xi
Sources	xiii
Performance Considerations	xv
Instruments	xix
Part Distribution	xxv

PART 1: THE ADORATION OF THE EARTH

Introduction *Beginning to 3 m. after reh. 21*	3
Introduction *Reh. 22 to Reh. 30*	5
Introduction *One before Reh. 35 to Reh. 48*	7
Spring Khorovod (Round Dance) *Reh. 49 to Reh. 54*	13
Games of the Rival Clans—Procession of the Wise Elder *Reh. 57 to Reh. 71*	17
Adoration Of The Earth (The Wise Elder) *4 m. before Reh. 72 to Reh. 72*	24
Dance Of The Earth *Reh. 72 to Reh. 79*	25

PART TWO: THE SACRIFICE

Introduction *Reh. 80 to one m. after Reh. 82*	33
Glorification Of The Chosen Victim *One m. after Reh. 103*	34
The Summoning Of The Ancients *One m. after Reh. 121 to Reh. 128*	42
Ritual of The Ancients *Reh. 128 to Reh. 131*	44
Ritual of the Ancients *Reh. 134 to Reh. 142*	46

Sacrificial Dance (The Chosen Victim) *Reh. 142 to Reh. 153*	51
Sacrificial Dance (The Chosen Victim) *Reh. 167 to Reh. 186*	58
Sacrificial Dance (The Chosen Victim) *Reh. 186 to the end*	62
Afterword	75
Endnotes	77
Bibliography	79
About the Author	81

ABBREVIATIONS

reh. = rehearsal number in score or part
m. = measure or measures

PREFACE

My first experience with *The Rite of Spring* was in 1996 at the Aspen Music Festival. Within three days of arriving to the almost two month festival, I fell off a bike and broke my collarbone. Obviously discouraged, I prepared to go back to Boston, but fortunately, was convinced to stay. During the festival, I learned the piece as best I could, conducting through the score and understanding the music without picking up a single mallet. When I was able to play again, I had a lesson with Ben Herman and Jonathan Haas. A couple weeks later, there were auditions to play the first timpani part on a concert with James Conlon. Somehow I won! My favorite comment that I still use today was "you'll be a legend in your own mind." Thanks?

A couple years later at the Schlewig-Holstein Musik Festival in Germany, *The Rite of Spring* was programmed for three concerts (the last at the Concertgebouw, arguably the most illustrious concert hall in the world) with Christoph Eschenbach. There would be an audition to play the first timpani part. To make things interesting, the drums to be used were set up German style (large drum on the right) and had calfskin heads. That was a first! For the American style players reading this, you have an idea of the challenge here. But somehow I got the part! Playing calfskin was a different animal (terrible, I know) and I appreciated the experience of dealing with its nuances and incredible sound.

While freelancing in Boston around 2000, the Boston Philharmonic performed *The Rite* a couple times and I got to tackle the much less interesting second timpani part.

It would be over ten years till I got to play *The Rite* again, this time with the Alexandria Symphony in VA for a couple performances on bass drum. The cycle is complete!

I wrote an article in grad school about the percussion section in *The Rite*. While I knew it needed some editing to be considered for a magazine publication, it had some legs. Over twenty years later (2020), I dug up the paper to see if it still had potential. I thought it did, so I typed each word into my computer, editing on the spot, adding, changing, and couldn't stop. What started as a potential seven-page article turned into twenty. Enter the rabbit hole! The more I researched, the longer it got. Add the musical examples, endless email threads, internet digging, score buying, phone conversations, general research, and it turned into what you're reading now.

While there are specific considerations for each percussion instrument, and they will all be discussed, there is a reason the timpani and bass drum parts are asked at most orchestra auditions. And there's a reason why they are some of the most talked about, dissected, and misunderstood parts in the literature. I hope this guide answers those questions.

If you're just learning the piece, I hope this helps in your preparation and appreciation of the music. For the professional, I hope it gives some historical insight, answers some questions about the many discrepancies in the scores and parts, and brings a new perspective into a future performance. At the least, I hope this will help the reader think about different ways to tackle the percussion parts with much more knowledge than when started.

Depending on whether you're reading on a device or paperback, I'd also suggest you follow a score or part as there isn't a musical example for each description. Larger versions of all the images can be viewed at:

www.chrisdechiara.com/riteofspringpics

I really appreciate the help of Mason Quinn and Clinton F. Nieweg for the endless emails, Dave Miller for the masterful engraving of some of the musical examples, Robert Schulz, Stephen Jones, Francesca Hurst, Doug Howard, and Russ Girsberger for more endless emails, keen eye, and wealth of experience.

Enjoy!

INTRODUCTION

The Rite of Spring

A Percussionist's Guide

Stravinsky's *The Rite of Spring* was premiered in Paris at the Théatres des Champs Élysées on May 29, 1913. It was the biggest theater scandal of the twentieth century, causing a riot that turned into a pivotal moment in music and ballet history. The music wasn't composed, but 'invented' and signaled the breakthrough of Modernism. While not revolutionary anymore or as difficult to perform, the piece changed classical music and percussion writing forever. Never before has a classical composer written anything like this and never before have we seen timpani and percussion parts written like this (except for maybe hints in Stravinsky's own *The Firebird* and *Petrouchka*). Dueling timpani parts, scraped tamtam, antique cymbals, addition of güiro, bass drum rhythms never seen before; it's a new world for the percussion section.

"When a man comes with a vision that is so new, so personal, and so traditional at the same time, how could one understand him? He sees what we don't see, he knows what we don't know. He understands what we do not understand, then little by little we follow and we can." (Nadia Boulanger)[1]

SOURCES

From Stravinsky's autograph score (unpublished except for a hard to find 2013 reprint) to the many editions that follow, we see the beginnings of where confusion can be had. The dates below indicate the year the edition was completed or published:

1911–1913: Sketches (published Boosey & Hawkes, 1969)
Cited in text as Sketches, 1911–13

1913: Autograph manuscript (lost)

1921: First published edition (based on 1913 autograph score)
Cited in text as RMV, 1921

1929: Revised edition
Le Sacre du printemps (Edited by F.H. Schneider)

1943: Revised version of Danse Sacrale
Cited in text as B+H, 1943

1947: Revised and corrected reprint of 1929 edition

1965: Corrected 1947 version

1967: Re-engraving of the 1947 edition
Cited in text as B+H, 1967

2000: Corrected 1921 edition (Edited by Clinton F. Nieweg)
Cited in text as Nieweg, 2000

2013: Reprint of 1913/1920 autograph
Cited in text as Autograph facsimile, 2013

Throughout these editions and handful of printed parts, there are countless revisions, printing and typographical mistakes, copyists' carelessness, publisher errors, and revisions by Stravinsky himself. Changes were made from its creation up until 1967, when Stravinsky gave his new publisher, Boosey & Hawkes, what he called the final version.

While we might think an original score to be the "holy grail," composers, especially Stravinsky, constantly revised his music based on performance situations, player suggestions, and his own whim. Perhaps this quote says it best:

"If the making of *The Rite*, of its music, scenario, and choreography, is complex and difficult to reconstruct, the stream of corrections, emendations, out-right rewritings and retractions that followed its initial performance is, regrettably, an even more tangled web of confusion, contradiction, and conflicting evidence." (Pieter Van den Toorn)[2]

PERFORMANCE CONSIDERATIONS

In some editions of the timpani part, there are roman numerals meant to dictate what drum is to be played at any given moment.

(Dover, 1965)

No matter the intention, it only takes into account the timpani that might've been available at the time. For instance, in some editions at 2 after reh. 106, the roman numeral "II" indicates the second drum down (a 25" or 26" drum today) be used for the D-sharp while the "I," the "smaller drum," (a 22" or 23" drum today) would be a *lower* pitch at B-sharp.

(Dover, 1965)

Is it because Stravinsky was considering the Timpani II part in the 11/4 bar before? There is an E-flat in the second drum (sometimes E-natural depending on the edition) and thus the player wouldn't have to change that drum's note. But the high F would have to be brought down to B-sharp ("drum I"). Drums were similar sizes in Stravinsky's time, so the difference between the "top two drum" sizes might not be as significant and a B-sharp could be easily done. While there are many other examples of this, they should be ignored as in the 2000 Nieweg edition (where I and II indicate which timpanist instead). Although it's interesting to know what Stravinsky was thinking, today's timpani are far more advanced and the tuning considerations would render the roman numeral approach obsolete.

Another consideration is the *a2* (for two) markings in the "Sacrificial Dance." In Nieweg's 2000 edition, starting at reh. 192 there are a2 markings over the *sforzando* As. While it might seem logical to double the *sforzando* As, the Cs also have the marking later. If you adhered to the editions with roman numerals, you'd have to play each note on two drums:

(Dover, 1965)

There are a few options for this:

1. Play with 2 mallets on each drum (not advised)
2. Two players play each note on one drum each
3. One person plays each note on two drums

It's consistent that Stravinsky at least means to double these notes in some fashion, most likely option 2—each player plays the note on one drum if possible. We could summarize that depending on the drums available, the timpanists will have to be aware of these considerations and how they will perform it. This subject will be presented in more detail when these passages appear.

Additionally, there were changes to the actual parts by conductor/percussionist and editor, Jean Morel. Morel is considered to be the timpanist that started editing these parts for himself, making them easier to perform. Originally, Stravinsky wrote many parts split between two timpanists. Since Morel's edits, it's common to play most of these parts by one person, leaving the 2nd timpanist with much less to do. Still, it's much easier and thus, more common, to perform passages such as this. It's unusual for a conductor to want the parts split up, but if they do, the timpanists will have to make sure their parts are as seamless as possible.

ORIGINAL SPLIT

(Dover, 1965)

COMBINED

(B+H, 1967)

INSTRUMENTS

Timpani (two players)

As mentioned above, the number of drums available and the timpanists' interpretation on how to play the part will determine how many drums are used and distributed. The easiest method is to have the 1st timpanist with a normal set of four drums, plus a piccolo drum placed so that the 2nd timpanist can share it. The 2nd timpanist will also have another drum used for the second half of the piece:

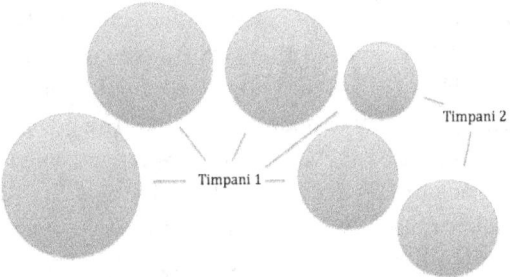

Another option is to have a set of five drums with an extra low drum that goes down to a low D-sharp (mentioned later), a piccolo timpano (shared), and at least two drums for the 2nd timpanist. This allows more flexibility between players and the ability for the 2nd timpanist to cover more notes if needed. This is one way I've performed it:

If enough drums are available, another option is to have a complete set for both timpanists. This will allow for the most flexibility and covering the *a2* parts in the "Sacrificial Dance":

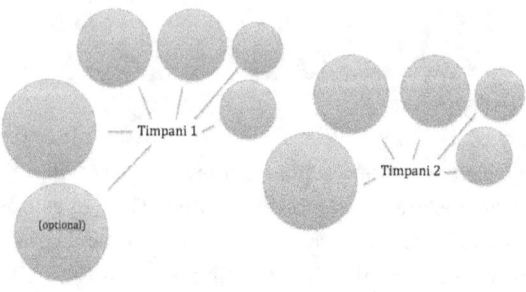

While calfskin heads have a far superior sound to plastic, you might not have a choice which heads you play on. Also, if you have to play German style (big drum to the right) AND with calfskin, and never have played that way, (this was my situation at the Schleswig-Holstein Musik Festival), it would behoove you to start practicing that way as soon as possible. The pedals won't be on the side you're used to, but at least you can get a sense of how the passages need to be performed, the stickings, etc. Also, since calf is so susceptible to weather and temperature changes, it's a good idea to get used to how the heads react to the pedaling. It might not be as accurate depending on the drum, head, and weather conditions. Developing a great sense of pedal feel, muscle memory, and pitch is essential.

For this guide, I'm writing with the American (largest drum on the left) set up in mind. Drum sizes aren't usually noted as so much will depend on the drums you're using. For instance, while a 32" drum might be mentioned, a 31" can work just fine, too.

Most tuning changes won't be discussed as it depends on the types of drums being used, the player's personal preference, and how the drums are split up with the 2nd timpanist.

Similarly, part interpretation and especially mallet choice will be the player's personal preference. Mallet choices are extremely personal, especially to the timpanist. A staccato sound for one passage could result in ten timpanists choosing 10 different pairs of mallets. All timpanists have wood mallets, but even these may differ in shape and size. In order to not damage the heads (especially calf), some timpanists will lightly wrap their wood mallets with a thin layer of felt, chamois, leather, etc.

Stravinsky calls for wood and regular mallets at certain times but no other specific stick anywhere else. While always a personal decision, it's up to the timpanist to use their best judgment on what the passage suggests. At least, the violent, hard, and dry sounds of the piece suggest different degrees of hard mallets be readily available.

Bass Drum

Assuming the drum is big enough to produce the sound required, the main considerations are:

- It can easily be laid flat to execute the beginning of "Dance of the Earth."
- A second drum is sometimes used, tuned to a B-flat. Usually this is a single headed drum. The autograph and 2000 editions are the only scores that have the bass drum part notated this way, although most parts do list the B-flat notation in at least one spot.

A wide variety of mallets are needed from soft and big; heavy and powerful. Some passages, including the popular passage at "Dance of the Earth," require a pair of hard or wood mallets (sometimes covered with chamois, leather, etc.).

Triangle

Since the triangle is played with a wooden stick (*bag. en bois*), the sonority isn't as important as the volume. Stravinsky indicates *fortissimo*, so the triangle should be large enough to produce a big sound. As with the antique cymbals, the triangle was added later and didn't appear in a score until the 1921 version.

Tambourine

The choice of instrument will be personal preference, but a drier tambourine is commonly used to help assist in the quiet dynamic needed.

Râpe guero

More commonly referred to as güiro. Since the part is played at a very loud volume, a large wooden or metal instrument can be used. Choose a scraping implement that will help produce a lot of volume, like a triangle beater or rattan stick. It's also common to use a washboard instead (triangle beater or brass mallets are effective) and sometimes to play more than one instrument with multiple players. Originally, this was written for bass drum. Güiro was added later and in some editions, at the end of the piece as well.

Antique cymbals (A-flat 5, B-flat 5)

Stravinsky had heard Debussy's *Prelude to "The Afternoon of a Faun"* in St. Petersburg in 1912, but was unaware of the tiny cymbals. He added them to his own orchestra later and they first appear in the 1921 version of the score.

Also known as crotales, antique cymbals should not be confused with finger cymbals. While antique cymbals have a specific pitch, finger cymbals do not. The proper octaves of the A-flat and B-flat should be adhered to and they should be struck with a triangle beater or brass mallet.

There are two common methods of mounting the cymbals:

- Each cymbal is tied to one end of a length of string. Hold the string in the middle so that each cymbal hangs evenly but does not touch. There can be a tendency for the cymbals to sway, so be care careful to not miss! It's also possible for each note to be played by a different percussionist.
- A more secure way is to mount the cymbals on a small stand specifically made for them, which will inhibit extraneous movement. Make sure there is nothing keeping them from resonating as much as possible.

In either case, a triangle beater or a mallet that produces a bright sound (like brass) will be appropriate.

Crash Cymbals
The choice of cymbals will be largely determined by the section at reh. 139. There needs to be enough volume at reh. 138, but comfortable enough to control for the immediate softer volume at reh. 139. A darker sound would fit the context of this section nicely. It's also possible to have a different player for each section.

Tam-Tam
While having two tam-tams is ideal, there are a few considerations:

- Since it needs to be scraped with a metal object, ideally there needs to be an area with a lot of friction. Depending on the kind of the tam-tam, scraping across the front surface or somewhere along the edge will work.
- In order to produce the fast, violent crescendo rolls and quick muffled notes, the instrument needs to be light/thin enough and of a size that allows it to react very quickly. Two smaller tam-tam mallets are needed.
- For the loud sections as in reh. 53, the tam-tam needs enough weight and size to produce a massive sound; same with the mallet used.

As noted later, it could be helpful to set up the tam-tam perpendicular to the stage. This way, you are facing the music, conductor, and can have a mallet on each side of the tam-tam for the rolls. This also helps for quicker and better muffling.

The 1921 score, based on the 1913 autograph, is the only score that has crash cymbals and güiro at the end of the "Sacrificial Dance."

(RMV, 1921)

The next published score came in 1929 in which the güiro and cymbals no longer appear at the end. In fact, they never again appear in any later edition.

In the 1943 revision of the "Sacrificial Dance," Stravinsky takes out the tam-tam and Timpani II parts completely. He also completely rewrites the Timpani I and bass drum parts.

Other pertinent changes will also be noted during the rest of this guide.

PART DISTRIBUTION

6-7 players
Timpani I
Timpani II (possible tambourine at 138)

Percussion 1
Bass Drum

Percussion 2
Tambourine
Güiro (or opt. Percussion 5)
Triangle or Antique Cymbals
Possible B-flat Bass Drum at 139

Percussion 3
Crash Cymbals (opt. suspended cymbal at end)
Güiro (or opt. Percussion 5)
Triangle or Antique Cymbals
Possible B-flat Bass Drum at 128 (or Percussion 4)

Percussion 4
Tam-Tam
Possible B-flat Bass Drum at 128 (or Percussion 3)

Percussion 5 (optional)
All B-flat Bass Drum parts
Güiro

5-6 Players
Timpani I
Timpani II, Tambourine at 138

Percussion 1
Bass Drum
Antique Cymbals or Triangle

Percussion 2
- Cymbals (opt. suspended at end)
- Antique Cymbals or Triangle
- Güiro (or opt. Percussion 4)
- Possible B-flat Bass Drum at 128

Percussion 3
- Tam-Tam
- Tambourine (except 138)
- Opt. Güiro at end
- Possible B-flat Bass Drum at 139

Percussion 4 (optional)
- All B-flat Bass Drum parts
- Güiro

PART 1: THE ADORATION OF THE EARTH

INTRODUCTION
BEGINNING TO 3 M. AFTER REH. 21

Among the many nerve-wracking moments of the piece for the 1st timpanist could be sitting and waiting for the first entrance. A solo with low strings, 8th note triplets from D to low G, concludes the buildup from the beginning of the piece. Depending on the tempo and if there is any kind of *ritard*, the 8th note triplet must be carefully placed and played confidently. The bass drum concludes the statement on beat 2 with the low strings and tuba. For the same reasons, this note needs to be placed perfectly after the timpanist's triplet. It looks like Stravinsky didn't originally intend there to be a bass drum note and was originally an 8th note. Sometimes it's written as a quarter note, so consult the tubas and basses to help determine how long this note should last.

4 | THE RITE OF SPRING

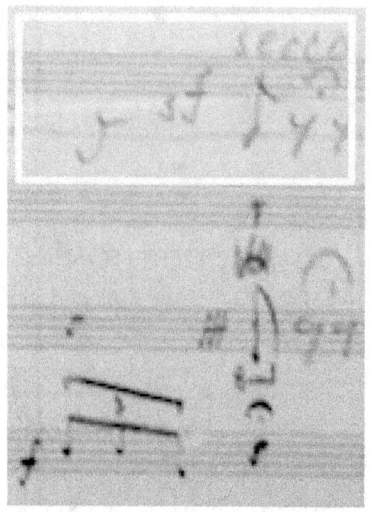

(Autograph facsimile, 2013)

In his sketches, it wasn't a complete triplet yet:

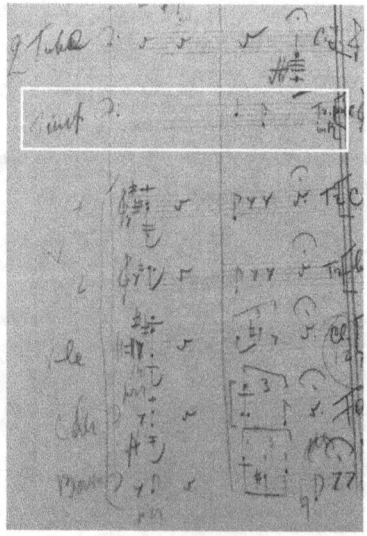

(Sketches, 1911-13)

INTRODUCTION
REH. 22 TO REH. 30

The next passage is the *pianissimo* timpani ostinato with the trombones at *mezzo forte*. In some scores, this is the first use of the seemingly useless roman numerals. Drums I, II, and III (top to bottom) represent E-flat, D-flat, and B-flat. As we'll see soon, these roman numerals can be ignored.

The timpani mallets needed for this passage require hardness that will make the rhythm speak, but soft enough to also produce a subtle, ominous sound:

(Dover, 1965)

In the 2000 edition, roman numerals indicate timpanist one and two:

(Nieweg, 2000)

Soon after, the triangle (*fortissimo*, played with wooden stick) and antique cymbals (*forte*, with triangle beater or brass mallet) enter on each beat:

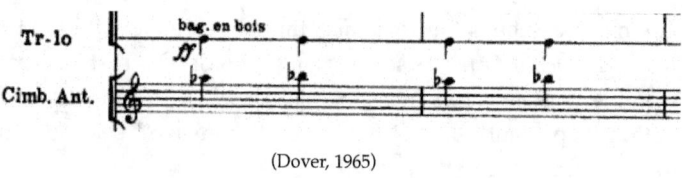

(Dover, 1965)

The timpani, triangle, and antique cymbal parts aren't found in his sketches (only timpani, bass drum, and piatti [crash cymbals] are listed), and appear sometime later in his 1920 revision.

INTRODUCTION
ONE BEFORE REH. 35 TO REH. 48

Four m. after reh. 34, the first timpanist's 8th notes have *secco* (dry, short) below them with accents:

(B+H, 1926)

These sound best when muffled on each rest as written. A big, fat, slightly hard stick will sound great. The goal is to match the intensity and power of the same notes everyone else plays. A great direction came from James Conlon, who suggested to play each group of two notes louder than each previous group, increasing the intensity leading to the "Ritual of Abduction."

At this point at reh. 37, it is critical that the percussionists quickly lock into the new tempo. Written at quarter note=132 bpm, it could be difficult to hear what the new tempo is if you were listening with no context or score; the timpani and bass drum seem to blast out of nowhere. Part of this is not only the sudden faster tempo, but the fact that everyone else is in 9/8. The timpanist and bass drummer have to think, not only in 3, but in a more duple, 3/4 feel *and* also play upbeats:

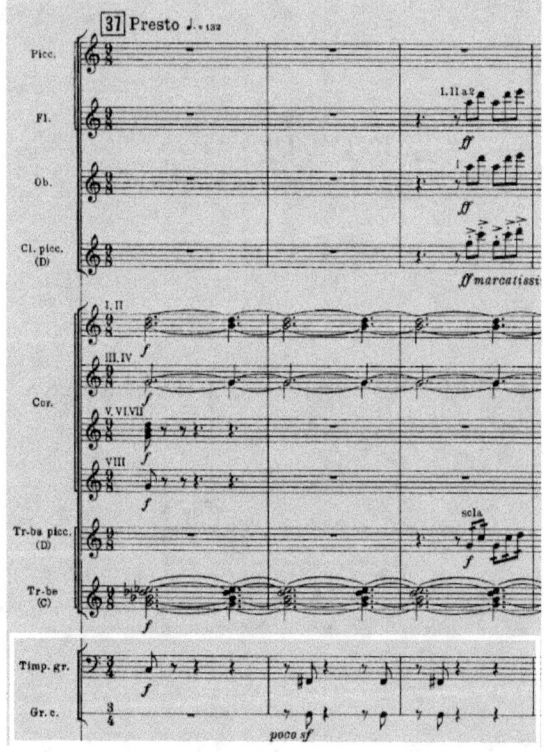

(Dover, 1965)

From the sketches, this was timpani only:

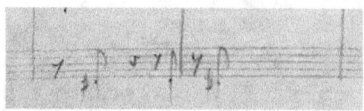

(Sketches 1911-1913)

In the next couple of measures, the timpani and low strings play a peculiar solo in a duple feel while still in 9/8. The way it's orchestrated will result in more of a timpani solo:

(Dover, 1965)

The way this passage is phrased makes it sound as if the "and" of 3 is the downbeat. The rhythm between the two drums has the feel of a modern day go-go groove:

The passage happens again before reh. 41, except beginning on the "and" of beat 1. A staccato mallet should be used for this section to assist in the secco marking and soloistic attitude. It's also possible to use two different sticks since the tension of a high B is much tighter than the lower C. Either way, make sure the high B isn't played too loudly and cause the phrase to be unbalanced. In some editions and most parts "baguettes dures et séches" is written two m. before reh. 44 (play with wood mallets). The 8th notes are a perfect example of "jumping on the train" and need to be played with direction and maybe a slight crescendo at the end:

(B+H, 1926)

It's interesting to see the original idea for this passage:

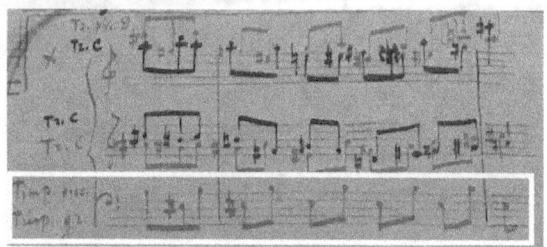

(Sketches, 1911-1913)

The "modo ordin." marked two before reh. 46 means "as usual":

(B+H, 1926)

Everything from reh. 38 to here was secco, so this note is to ring—and to be explosive.

During the upcoming passages, a solid sense of time is necessary. So, I prefer to play the G-sharp on the second low drum (32" when I used this set up) and then the F on the regular 32" drum within the setup. While it's certainly easy to tune from the G-sharp to F on one drum, the second low drum helps this passage and upcoming passages as well. With timpani playing in general, one usually plays the notes needed on the drum that produces that note the best. At the same time, in *The Rite*, there are some quick tuning changes and no time for listening to your tuning. This is where knowing your drums and the feel of the pedals come into play. Tuning gauges help, but with pitch changing throughout a performance due to climate (especially calf) and the orchestra pitch going up or down, you have to ultimately rely on your ears.

From reh. 46–47, it's of utmost importance to make sure you know how the conductor is subdividing all these sections so you can mark them in your part for accuracy. These notes sound good with a mallet that produces a violent, sharp (not in pitch!), immediate attack, still with good tone. Care needs to be taken not to carelessly play these notes and sharpen the pitch or knock the drum out of tune. Constantly subdivide 8th notes in this section.

Six measures before reh. 48, the bass drum and timpani trade blows, the bass drum note a true solo—make it big. In the autograph score, Stravinsky originally intended this to be timpani. He then added bass drum:

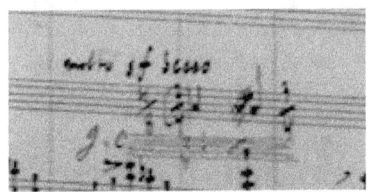

(Autograph facsimile, 2013)

Later, he took out the timpani note from beat 1. In this case, secco means short:

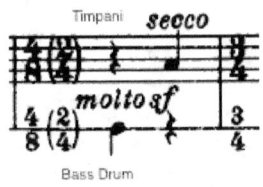

(Dover, 1965)

The following timpani notes, and everyone but strings, play a 3-2 clave pattern, but most likely unintentional. They're notated with "sim." under them, referring to secco a couple measures previously. So these notes need to be short as everyone else in the orchestra:

12 | THE RITE OF SPRING

(Dover, 1965)

SPRING KHOROVOD (ROUND DANCE)
REH. 49 TO REH. 54

At reh. 49, the first bass drum note, with low winds and strings, is crucial in introducing this new world of sound:

14 | THE RITE OF SPRING

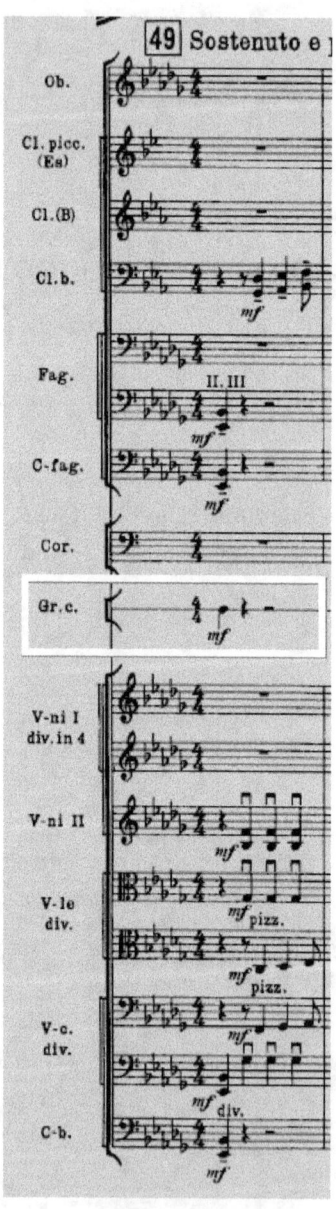

(Dover, 1965)

Spring Khorovod (Round Dance) | 15

Although *mezzo forte*, it still needs a big, round sound, as if being swallowed up into the Earth. Put weight behind it and imitate the low string sound. A large, soft, but heavier mallet played off center would help produce a nice and big dark tone. Also be sure to muffle accordingly, most likely after two full beats.

In Stravinsky's sketches, this was only timpani on B-flat and E-flat:

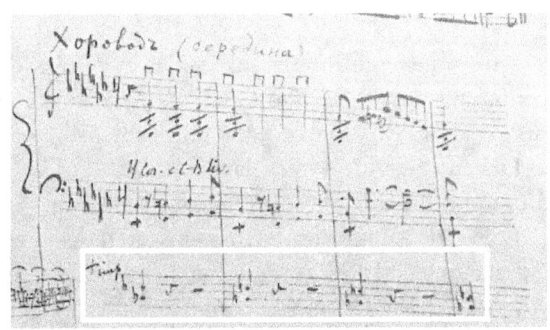

(Sketches, 1911-1913)

At reh. 53, the tam-tam and timpani enter:

(Dover, 1965)

The timpani have three grace notes that crescendo to the *forte* downbeat. The grace notes can be interpreted in many ways. One guideline is to follow what Stravinsky mentions: "...the timpanist appogiuture [*sic*] should be heard as three distinct notes."[3] This statement suggests the timpanist should play in a much more open style than how a 4-stroke ruff on a snare drum would usually be played (much closer together). James Conlon instructed me to play them almost as a 16th note triplet starting on the 8th note before:

However it's interpreted, the timpanist and bass drummer should communicate so that the bass drummer can place their downbeats accordingly. At reh. 53, the notes are also marked *assai* (very), so this can be BIG. Some players play the grace notes on the 32" drum and the downbeat on the adjacent drum. This separates the figure for a more powerful, separate attack, especially since the grace notes that high in the range of the low drum will speak a lot more clearly. If your bottom drum doesn't get a B-flat, then using only one drum is perfectly fine. If it does, there also could be a problem of intonation.

The B-flat on a 32" or 31" is extremely high in that range, but in the middle range of the adjacent drum. Make sure both drums sound perfectly in tune with each other before attempting this method. You can also muffle the bottom B-flat as soon as you play the upper B-flat.

The timpani notes between reh. 54–56 are all short punctuations with the orchestra. Make sure to muffle quickly and stay on top of the beat. The bass drum at reh. 55, with its' tenuto markings, can be played longer (but with good attack) like the basses.

GAMES OF THE RIVAL CLANS—
PROCESSION OF THE WISE ELDER
REH. 57 TO REH. 71

At the beginning of the "Ritual of the Two Rival Tribes," the timpanist has one and a half beats to lock into the new tempo of quarter note=166 bpm and land the rhythm perfectly with the tuba. Originally, Stravinsky wrote only notes that followed the tuba part and later revised the passage to include both tuba parts:

(RMV, 1921)

Revised, with added Cs (instead of F#s), the high B can be played by the 1st timpanist for cleaner ensemble:

(B+H, 1967)

Similarly, three m. and one m. before reh. 59 require complete mastery and no hesitation. Before each entrance, the tempo slows to about 55—60 bpm and immediately jumps back into tempo for the timpani and tuba solos. Notice how Stravinsky leaves out the downbeat two before reh. 59. This leaves the listener's expectations suspended at the next mysterious bar. The downbeat at reh. 59 punctuates the phrase and pushes everyone forward:

(Dover, 1965)

Before this passage, at two m. before reh. 58, the timpani play 8th notes with the trumpets, but the tubas play half notes. The question is whether to muffle on the "and" of beat 3 or let the drum ring until the next beat or bar. It's always a good idea to ask the players how they're interpreting their parts:

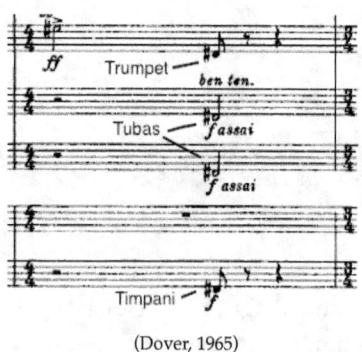

(Dover, 1965)

Everyone has the same driving rhythm three m. before reh. 61 starting on beat 2, but the passage sounds like it might begin on beat 1:

Games of the Rival Clans—Procession of the Wise Elder | 19

(Dover, 1965)

In Stravinsky's sketches, the passage indeed starts on beat 1 and with the following 8th notes in the opposite direction:

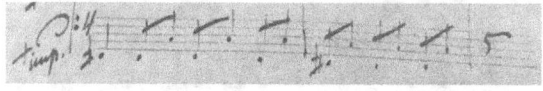

(Sketches, 1911-1913)

In later editions, the terms *détaché* (in this case a more aggressive form of staccato—see markings over each note) and *non troppo* (not too much) appear.

The bass drum entrance three m. before reh. 65 is marked secco so some type of muffling technique should be involved in getting a drier sound, but still *big*. This constant space between each quarter note suggests Stravinsky is thinking in cut time:

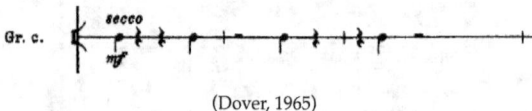

(Dover, 1965)

Although still in four, this rhythm gives the impression of a different meter occurring during the straight four by the rest of the orchestra.

The addition of the 8th notes in the timpani at reh. 67 will help keep the pulse steady. Editions and parts differ on whether there are staccato markings over each note and as to what the dynamic is. A good *mezzo piano* to *mezzo forte* will suffice:

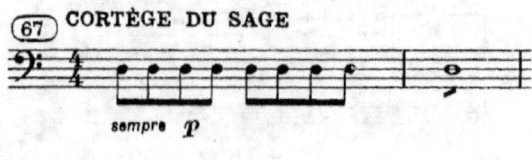

(Dover, 1965)

Games of the Rival Clans—Procession of the Wise Elder | 21

The tam-tam enters with a three bar phrase starting on the "and" of 1. This produces a slow two feel with the bass drum (as indicated in the upcoming 6/4 section). The equal spacing of the tam-tam and bass drum adds another two feel, except not starting on beat 1. It's as if the tam-tam was on beat 1 and the bass drum on beat 2. It can also be felt as a syncopated waltz against the quarter note pulse:

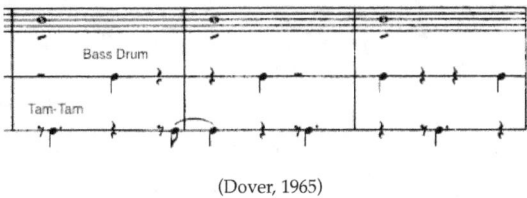

(Dover, 1965)

It might be a good idea to muffle every tam-tam note on the following quarter rests so that every entrance has a better chance of being present.

Since Stravinsky didn't originally write a tam-tam part, the instrument was yet to be determined:

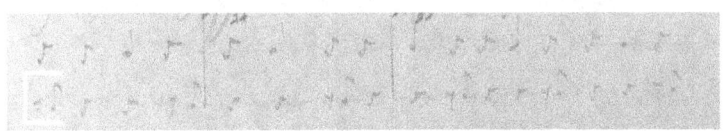

(Sketches, 1911-1913)

Starting at reh. 70, the timpani accent every fourth 8th note, in conjunction with the pattern of the previous bass drum and tam-tam rhythms. This strengthens the impression of a slow four feel over the new 6/4 phrased bars by the rest of the orchestra. It can also be thought of as a 2:3 or 3:2 polyrhythm in each half of the bar. The bass drum and tam-tam continue their pattern except now notated and grouped in duple time within the 6/4 meter, lining up with the accents of the timpani. Originally written for bass drum, the güiro enters with what could very well be the hardest part of this section.

There is also no dynamic listed in any edition except the 2000 Nieweg:

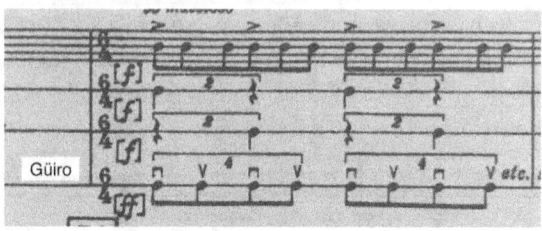

(Nieweg, 2000)

Originally there were either two bass drum parts intended (one with wooden stick) or Stravinsky meant for one player to play the rim and the head. But in either case, there was no güiro thought of yet:

(Sketches, 1911-1913)

In 1913, Stravinsky came across the güiro with the help of Ravel, who took him to a percussionist with a collection of the instruments, or as Stravinsky called them, "cheese graters." He did permit the substitution of Mexican gourds and bean pods when they were louder than the güiro. Today, the most cutting sound is produced by using a small washboard scraped with a hard mallet (triangle beater, brass mallet, etc). Sometimes, the part is doubled. Stravinsky "wants this part to be heard over the whole orchestra especially the second and fourth scratches in the group"[4] even though that seems to be the other way around in the "bowing" marks. Each 8th note is marked "down, up, down, up," etc.) Normally, a "down bow" would have more emphasis than an "up bow." So if he wanted every second and fourth 8th note to be stronger, he should've written the down bows over those notes instead.

To execute the rhythm precisely, there are several ways to think about it:

- Fit within the dotted half notes of the bar.
- Fit into the duple time of the bass drum and tam-tam (this also produces a fast 2:3 polyrhythm with the timpani).
- Ignore the other parts, keep subdividing quarter notes, and think of the performed rhythm as constant dotted 8th-16ths; a 4:3 polyrhythm:

Did Stravinsky compose the first rock beat that evolves from the güiro, tam-tam, and bass drum parts?

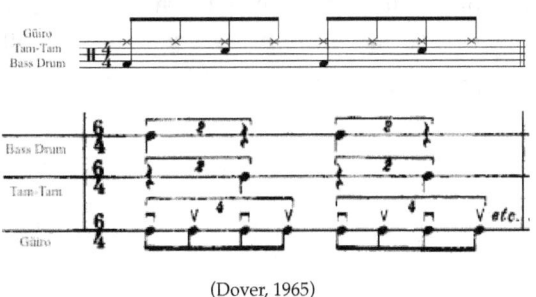

(Dover, 1965)

ADORATION OF THE EARTH (THE WISE ELDER)
4 M. BEFORE REH. 72 TO REH. 72

A quick change to a softer timpani mallet would be appropriate for the 8th notes 4 m. before reh. 72; the 'creaking of the old Sage's knees.'

(Dover, 1965)

At this slower tempo, a sensitive touch and timing are important to match the character and placement of the same 8th notes in the basses and contra bassoon.

DANCE OF THE EARTH
REH. 72 TO REH. 79

The bass drum passage at reh. 72 is on virtually every orchestra audition:

(B+H, 1926)

A common way to perform this passage is to have the bass drum lying flat or tilted and muffled enough so that it can be played with extreme rhythmic precision. Many professional percussionists have made mallets (wood, aluminum, sometimes covered with leather, etc.) to execute this passage with the proper articulation. For the first two measures, Robert Craft (Stravinsky's longtime assistant, author, and conductor) states, "The 1st note of each triplet in the bass drum part (wood sticks) should be accented."[5]

The player has one beat to lock into the new tempo. The crescendo should be as loud as possible, but the downbeat of the third measure has to be *piano*. One common way is to alternate every triplet note, then play four 16th notes and an 8th note, the peak being the 3rd note of the triplet. Another is to play a quintuplet on the 3rd beat:

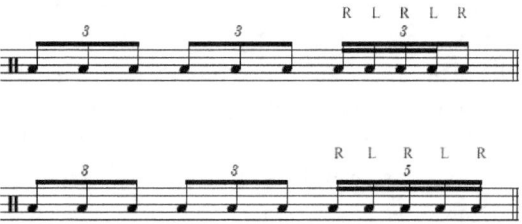

The first example allows for better rhythmic accuracy, a violent/precise crescendo, and being able to come down in volume for the downbeat. If all goes well, the left hand should hit on the downbeat of the 3rd measure (if starting with the right hand). In the 3rd measure on beat 2, the *sforzando* accent should end up on the right hand. Originally in his sketches, the figure started as one measure of 16th notes, then 16th notes for the whole section, not triplets:

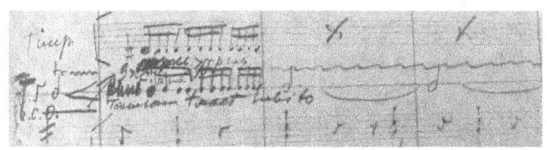

(Sketches, 1911-1913)

In the 7th and 8th measures of this section, the bass drum has similar figures, except now in the second measure it's recommended to play beat 2 as RLL so you can start the roll with the right as before.

Throughout this passage, all *sforzando* markings are within the *fortissimo* dynamic. Make sure the 8th notes are not too soft and keep the triplet feel by *slightly* pulsing the downbeats. The *piano* dynamic needs to be enough where the *crescendo* and drop to *subito piano* at reh. 75 is very effective.

Also noted in the above part are reminders of where your hands should be following on the downbeats of each bar. These will help keep your place and make sure your hands are lining up where they should.

Even though the tam-tam has been introduced already with a common playing technique (in terms of *how* it's played), the upcoming passages introduce techniques never seen or heard before in the orchestral literature: scraping, quick dampening, and short, two-handed crescendo rolls.

In the second measure of "Dance of the Earth," the tam-tam assists in the bass drum roll crescendo with a huge, violent roll. Two mallets are best and positioning yourself in such a way to have total control of the tam-tam is of utmost importance. I find that the easiest way for a roll like this is to have the tam-tam facing perpendicular to the stage like a bass drum. This way you can muffle the tam-tam quickly with your hand, arms, or legs while rolling on each side of the tam-tam. You're also facing the music and the conductor, so you never have to turn in any other direction. If this is not possible, it can be helpful for someone not playing to also muffle. In either case, choose a tam-tam that will speak quickly and loudly!

The 1st timpanist comes in with its opposing rhythm of 16th notes (marked *bien net*—loosely translated as clean and precise) adding to the tension and buildup to the end of this half of the piece. It might be a good idea to muffle the F-sharp for better rhythmic clarity as the C will have no trouble in that range (assuming the C is on the adjacent drum). Throughout this section, it's a good idea to mark cues of the trumpet entrances so you know where you should be lining up in the measures they play. At reh. 78, the timpani immediately switch from 16ths to 8th note triplets, while the bass drum switches from 8th note triplets to duple 8th notes:

(Dover, 1965)

Three after reh. 78, the notes keep diminishing with the timpani down to 8th notes. "The 8th note rhythm, in the timpani toward the end of the "Dance" must be heard."[6] The bass drum diminishes to quarter notes to the end of the first half. A common practice is to let off of the bass drum muffling near where the quarter notes enter, possibly changing to a bigger mallet.

This allows for more power and resonance to the notes, especially if played with one hand till the end:

(Dover, 1965)

PART TWO: THE SACRIFICE

INTRODUCTION
REH. 80 TO ONE M. AFTER REH. 82

The timpani rolls at reh. 80 should be with soft sticks that produce a full, round sound:

(Dover, 1965)

Depending on the edition, the rolls are notated for the 1st timpanist on A and the 2nd timpanist on D. Stravinsky originally wrote the rolls for one person, but two mallets on one drum sound much better than a single mallet on each drum. Each timpanist must carefully start their rolls at precisely the same time, considering the slow tempo. The bass drum rolls should be as smooth as possible without any accent on the downbeats.

GLORIFICATION OF THE CHOSEN VICTIM
ONE M. AFTER REH. 103

The famous 11/4 measure introducing "Glorification of the Chosen Victim" is one of the most famous moments in musical history. Some even call it the beginning of heavy metal:

Glorification Of The Chosen Victim | 35

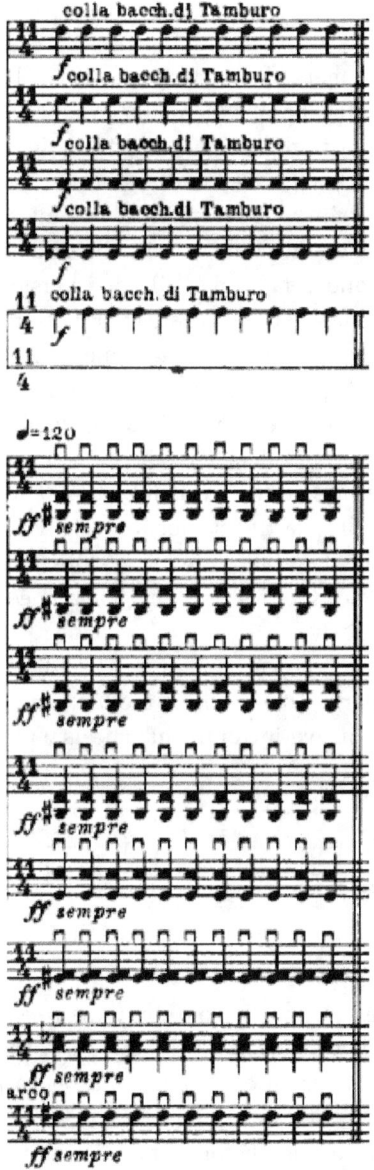

(Dover, 1965)

While the bar is marked at quarter note=120 bpm, tempi have ranged from 60-160 bpm! No matter what the tempo is, both timpani and bass drum need to be perfectly in synch with every note and watching what the conductor does. Each instrument is directed to play with wooden mallets, but this could end up as personal preference. In some scores, the 2nd timpanist's notes have E-natural and F-natural while one version, including the autograph score, has an E-flat. There are E-flats in the celli, so play an E-flat. This discrepancy has existed since 1913.

The measure is preceded by a violent scrape of the tam-tam. There are many ways to execute this, some being a triangle beater, screwdriver, or even pliers. As mentioned earlier, it's worth exploring the surface of the tam-tam to make sure to find the best spot to produce an effective scrape, especially at the peak of the crescendo. "[T]he tam-tam must be 'stopped' on its concave side…"[7] Sometimes this rest is short, sometimes long, so always best to muffle quickly.

In the next section, each measure's subdivisions need to be marked in the parts. This is where the tuba and timpani are best friends, with the answering of the tuba beats with the timpani As:

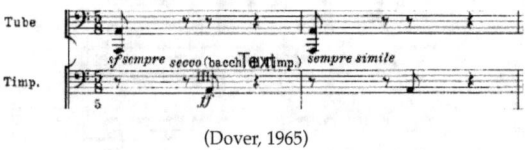

(Dover, 1965)

Since these notes are mostly solo (only the basses play the same note an octave lower) and they follow an A from the tuba, it's imperative that the drum chosen gets the best A possible, played with good tone, but still forceful.

The 9/8 measure one before reh. 105 could have just been a 3/4 and 3/8 bar since everyone is playing some sort of duple rhythm. The bass drum and low strings are the only instruments playing on the beat, but in some scores, the bass drum part has been written on the upbeats. Both times should be performed on the beat:

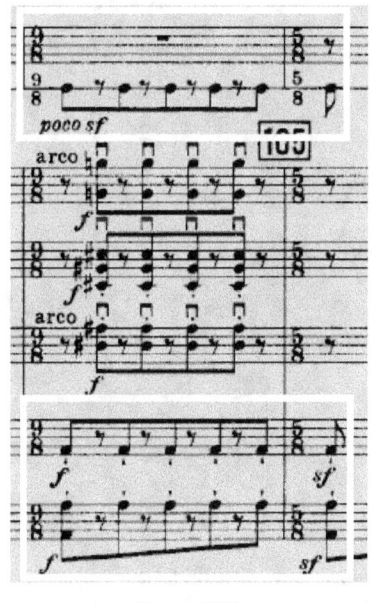

(Dover, 1965)

It's best to keep the 8th note steady in your head while playing quarter notes, whether or not you muffle on the 8ths, and to not rush. The *poco sforzandos* are for ALL notes, not just the downbeat. In general, this section is where the timpani and bass drum need to lock in perfectly with the conductor. Any slight wavering of rhythm spoils the effect of each instrument's placement.

As mentioned earlier, some score editions have roman numerals dictating which drum to play in the timpani part. One measure after reh. 106 (and the 11/4 bar), this can be ignored for the same reasons discussed earlier. From low to high, the drums will be tuned F-sharp, A, B-sharp, D-sharp.

From reh. 106–109, the autograph score directs the bass drum, "*Frotter avec una brosse*" (rub with a [wire] brush):

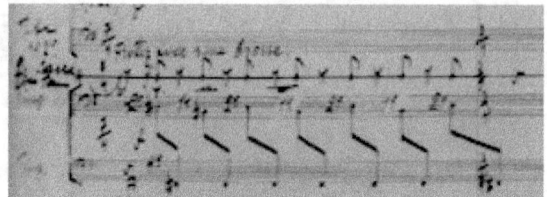

(Autograph facsimile, 2013)

In the measure before, instead of a scrape of the tam-tam, Stravinsky wrote a roll on the bass drum with a "thin" stick:

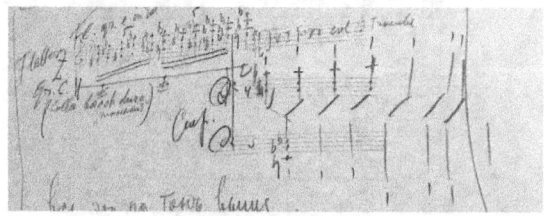

(Sketches, 1911-1913)

The timpani part only had two notes (notated E-sharp and F-natural an octave apart) in the sketches:

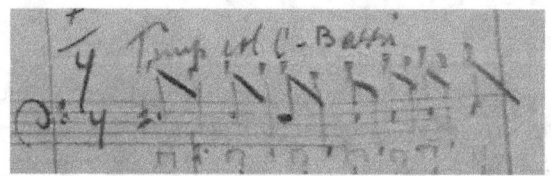

(Sketches, 1911-1913)

At reh. 111, the solo bass drum notes are written as 8th notes, but should ring instead:

(B+H, 1926)

Glorification Of The Chosen Victim | 39

A large, somewhat soft mallet capable of producing a big, deep, guttural blow would work nice here. They should also be some of the biggest notes you ever play on the instrument.

In the 1st timpani part (with wood mallets) one m. before reh. 113, the drums are better tuned: 32" as a G-flat (will stay from previous F-sharp), 29" at an F and the high F on the 26":

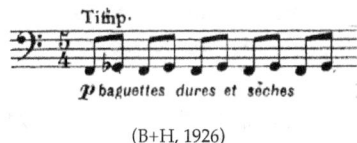

(B+H, 1926)

This allows for less tuning and easier flow and motion at reh. 114, with no cross-over sticking:

(B+H, 1926)

Change from wood to a softer mallet with plenty of articulation. Even though the time signature changes throughout this passage at reh. 114, it's best to count how many times the ostinato happens (high F as each downbeat) instead of trying to follow the conductor; there will be 24 *complete* groups. The accent on the low F must be brought out to compensate for the more projected sound of the high F. Christoph Eschenbach had me play this section very soloistically, around a *mezzo forte* with *forte* accents.

There are discrepancies in different editions as to what kind of mallets are needed and where to play on the bass drum before reh. 113. Some editions notate "bacch. di timp." (timpani mallet, but wood is commonly used here), but not where to play on the drum. Some editions notate "au bord" (edge of head) and some don't say anything. At reh. 114, it's consistent that the edge of the head is to be played (even the autographed score notates this), but again it says with a timpani mallet. In this section, muffle the 8th notes enough so that they're clearly heard:

(RMV, 1921)

As mentioned before, at one m. before reh. 118, the bass drum has the similar 9/8 bar as one m. before reh. 105, except now the 8th notes are incorrectly notated as upbeats:

Glorification Of The Chosen Victim | 41

(Dover, 1965)

Stravinsky changed this in 1947 and it since has been notated on the beat with the strings as before.

THE SUMMONING OF THE ANCIENTS
ONE M. AFTER REH. 121 TO REH. 128

In the measure after reh. 121, the 2nd timpanist should play the high F-sharp, leaving the 1st timpanist to execute their own notes. (The 2000 Nieweg edition indicates I and II as players one and two.) In 1962, Stravinsky changed the rhythm of the bass notes from two 8th notes and a quarter to a quarter note triplet: F-sharp, E, D-sharp. The timpani part should match if so.

No matter what the timpanist has in their part, they should be aware of what the bassists are playing and try to match. Sometimes it's the same pitches (F-sharp, E, D-sharp), but as two 8th notes and a quarter note. This is another spot where the extra low drum will come in handy: (29")-F-sharp, (32")-E, and second (32")-D-sharp. If the tuning can be managed, it's also possible to play a low F-sharp and then the higher E to D-sharp. Here are some of the options:

The Summoning Of The Ancients | 43

The preceding timpani rolls are the only sounds that cut off before the next downbeat (and can also be played by the 2nd timpanist instead). Perhaps Stravinsky was aware of the timpanist having to move to the other drums and that it would be impossible to fill the roll to the following downbeats. Careful counting is required during this "jazzy" section, with the quick meter changes in a "one" feel into the 3/2 bars. Since the quarter note is constant, subdivide them throughout.

Set up the bass drum so that the biggest, smoothest rolls can be achieved. Ideally, it'll be laid flat for the most control and volume. Be sure to count so that the punctuations at the end of the rolls are precise.

RITUAL OF THE ANCIENTS
REH. 128 TO REH. 131

At reh. 128, there must be perfect ensemble for the little march between the bass drum, timpani, and the tambourine; it's first appearance:

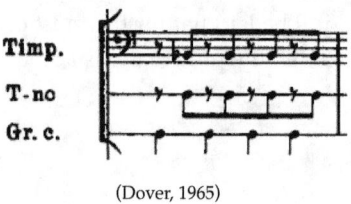

(Dover, 1965)

Even though this seems like a completely new tempo, it's very common that the previous quarter note will equal the 16th note. Subdividing this way should help make the first measure at reh. 128 much more precise.

The sound of the tambourine tending to be on the late side, the player should anticipate and play on top of the beat, even in this slow tempo.

Each instrument, while playing a *piano* dynamic, needs to match in volume without a single instrument sticking out of the texture.

This is also where the infamous "B-flat bass drum" part is sometimes notated. The 2000 Nieweg score edition is the only score that includes this note, but there are various bass drum parts where it appears:

(B+H, 1926)

The part is directed *"avec la baguette de bois touchez au bord façon à produire un Si-flat environ"* which means to play the drum with a wood stick near the edge, approximately producing the note of B-flat. This was written later into the autograph score, most likely to mimic the plucking of the B-flats in the celli and the tuning of the timpani. They're also written as quarter notes (sometimes with a staccato over them), so it's best to muffle on the offbeats where the timpani and tambourine play. If it will be performed with a second bass drum, and the switch to the B-flat isn't possible by the main bass drummer, either the cymbal or tam-tam player should cover this part. If an added percussionist is used, they can play all the B-flat bass drum parts.

In many of the original sketches, this section looks quite different; timpani and percussion (bass drum, tam-tam, cymbals) started as quarter notes. Also, the B-flat bass drum idea was there from the beginning and there are no upbeats for percussion until later:

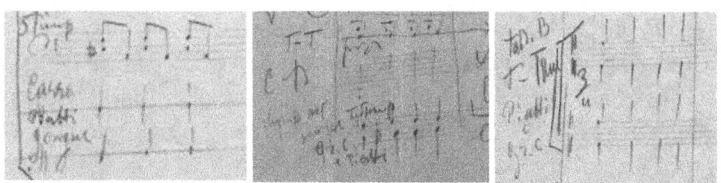

(Sketches, 1911-1913)

RITUAL OF THE ANCIENTS
REH. 134 TO REH. 142

At reh. 134, even though the whole orchestra is playing at least *forte*, only *piano* is written in the timpani parts:

(Dover, 1965)

Robert Craft mentioned that at reh. 134 and the upcoming section at reh. 138, the timpani are best played by one player with a "stick shaped like a 3-pronged candelabra which can poise and roll over all three drum heads."[8] The four-mallet marimba grip didn't exist in 1913, so Stravinsky or Craft came up with the three-pronged mallet idea. This still doesn't make a lot of sense at reh. 134 since the G and D can be played with two hands, and the high B by the 2nd timpanist. And he specifically notates it that way. At reh. 138, it might make more sense, but there still needs to be five notes played at the same time:

Ritual of the Ancients | 47

(Dover, 1965)

There are several ways to interpret this section depending on how many drums and players are being used. Considering the 1st timpanist's challenges following this section after 139, they should either play the G and D or G and B-flat only. The 2nd timpanist (with two mallets in one hand) can play either the B-flat, F, and high B-natural or D, F, and high B-natural. If there are only three percussionists available, the 2nd timpanist could play the F, high B, and tambourine. That would still leave the 1st timpanist having to play three notes and also the delicate B-flat notes at reh. 140 with one hand. If so, the 2nd timpanist could play the offbeat Ds. This would still leave the 1st timpanist to possibly place three mallets down and pick up another for the entrance soon after reh. 142. Ideally, there will be someone available to play tambourine and eliminate this issue.

From reh. 136–137 of the autograph score, Stravinsky writes high F-natural punctuations with the rest of the orchestra:

(Autograph facsimile, 2013)

Stravinsky writes curious dynamics at reh. 138. While the whole orchestra is playing at least *forte*, the timpanists play *mezzo piano*, tambourine-*piano*, tam-tam-*mezzo forte*, bass drum-*forte*, and the loudest instrument, the crash cymbals (their first appearance) at *fortissimo*. This is another place that's best decided amongst the section and conductor. Even though all the notes for the percussionists are written as 8th notes, it should also be decided on what makes more musical sense, to let ring or muffle on each 8th rest.

At reh. 138, the bass drummer needs to play with one regular mallet while holding a wood mallet in the other for the quarter notes at reh. 139. But in the autograph score, Stravinsky notes that reh. 139 be played on the B-flat drum again (although he doesn't designate to play on the edge):

Ritual of the Ancients | 49

(Autograph facsimile, 2013)

If this is the case, another player should play this part as before (see part divisions at beginning). At reh. 140, the regular bass drum is played again with a regular mallet (G-C is short for Gran Cassa):

(B+H, 1926)

For the sake of clarity, and if two bass drums are being used:

128: B-flat drum, near edge with wooden mallet
138: Regular drum, beating area, and mallet
139: B-flat drum (autograph score), regular beating spot, wood mallet
140: Regular drum, beating area, and mallet

During the delicate passage at reh. 139, the cymbal player needs to make quite an effort to come down to *piano* right after the *fortissimo* notes. One option is to have smaller cymbals for the whole passage starting at reh. 138, as long as they produce a loud enough volume. This will make it easier to control at reh. 139. It would also help to slightly muffle the last note before reh. 139 and play it as a 16th note or just muffle on the "and" of beat 4. It also needs to be determined whether or not the 8th notes should ring or not. At the soft dynamic, letting them ring most likely would not interfere with anything else being played. A final option is another percussionist plays the loud or soft section.

The 1st timpanist plays an unusual passage with 8th notes in the left hand on a B-flat and a double stop on the upbeats with the right hand on D. The left hand is notated with each 8th note alternating between *piano* and *pianissimo*, while the right hand on D is maintaining *pianissimo*. If these dynamics are specifically adhered to, it might help if the 2nd timpanist play the D upbeats and the 1st timpanist stay on the B-flats.

SACRIFICIAL DANCE (THE CHOSEN VICTIM)
REH. 142 TO REH. 153

In the "Sacrificial Dance," the most important thing the timpanist can do besides be perfectly in tune, is to *count*. Subdividing 16th notes is the key. An articulate mallet with a lot of clarity will punctuate the spaces well. The part went through many changes through the '20s and into the '40s. There were countless note addition/discrepancies heard on recordings between reh. 142–147 and 167–172. None of these were in any printed score or part. Most notable is one m. before reh. 146 and one m. before reh. 171. Before the timpani motive starts each time, some timpanists played two additional notes to lead off the section:

The same option applies to the C-sharp and E before reh. 171. There are many recordings containing these motives (and other notes) being played, but it's more common to leave them out and play what is normally on the printed part. When Stravinsky was asked directly if these notes should be played, Stravinsky replied "<u>No</u>, they shall <u>not</u>."[9]

Each entrance must be perfectly placed as most of them are solos or with the basses only, fitting in between the syncopated rhythms of the orchestra:

(Dover, 1965)

Know the music well enough that you can *hear* where the notes fall instead of solely relying on what you see.

At reh. 146, the timpani and basses play this rhythmically precise solo together in a hocket fashion with the orchestra. Subdivide 16th notes, not only before your entrance, but also while playing:

Sacrificial Dance (The Chosen Victim)

(Dover, 1965)

In the third measure of reh. 148, make sure to count even harder as to not come in early with the F in the 2/8 bar:

(Dover, 1965)

In reh. 146 of the autographed score (and 1921), the timpani part is much less involved, including occasional octave Fs and bass drum notes instead:

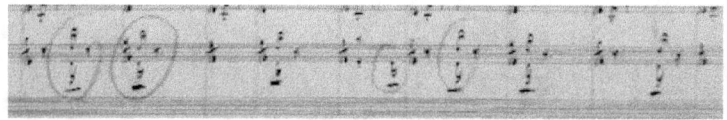

(Autograph facsimile, 2013)

In the 1943 revision of the "Sacrificial Dance," some of the timpani notes are replaced with bass drum:

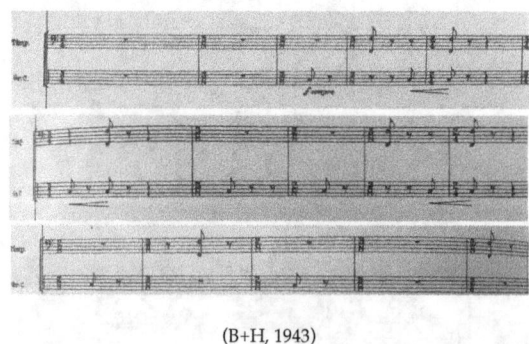

(B+H, 1943)

Three m. before reh. 153, the tam-tam violently scrapes again into another big, true solo for the timpanist:

Sacrificial Dance (The Chosen Victim) | 57

(B+H, 1926)

Make the timpani solo big and muffle all four notes as quickly as possible:

(Dover, 1965)

SACRIFICIAL DANCE (THE CHOSEN VICTIM)

REH. 167 TO REH. 186

One m. after reh. 171 in the autograph score (now reh. 171), Stravinsky writes all E's instead of C-sharp to E:

(Autograph facsimile, 2013)

He later changed to the bass line:

(B+H, 1926)

After the timpani and basses play this solo again (sometimes erroneously listed in the 1926 Timpani II part), the bass drum introduces the next section with syncopated notes, which also need to be perfectly placed between the orchestra's rhythms in the second and fourth measure. Similar to the timpani before reh. 149, the bass drum has the same rhythm before reh. 174. Don't be early on the last (solo) note of the 2/8 measure:

Sacrificial Dance (The Chosen Victim) | 59

(Dover, 1965)

At reh. 174 (some conductors insert a fermata before starting this section), the percussion section is sort of a percussion ensemble, each instrument filling in the rests of another instrument, producing a constant, raucous stream of notes. Different editions can be interpreted as having the 1st timpanist playing the low F and B-flat, the 2nd timpanist a high F, E-flat, and B-flat:

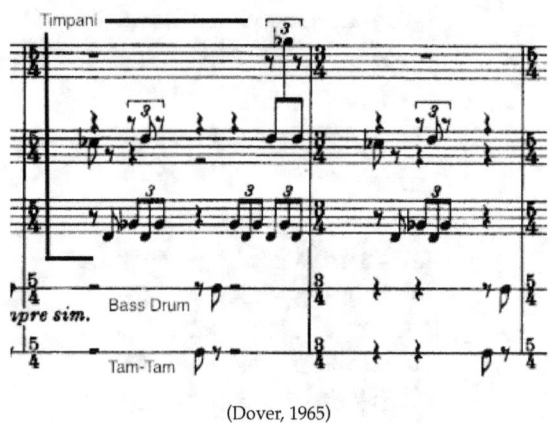

(Dover, 1965)

For rhythmic accuracy, the E-flat is usually played and written into the 1st timpanist's part, leaving the 2nd timpanist with just the F and high B-flat (the only note change for the piccolo drum):

(B+H, 1926)

Even though he kept the scrape before the timpani solo prior to reh. 153, as stated earlier, the 1943 revision by Stravinsky contains a completely rewritten timpani and bass drum part. He also leaves out the Timpani II and tam-tam parts altogether:

Sacrificial Dance (The Chosen Victim) | 61

(B+H, 1943)

In his sketches, the bass drum had two grace notes before some of the beats:

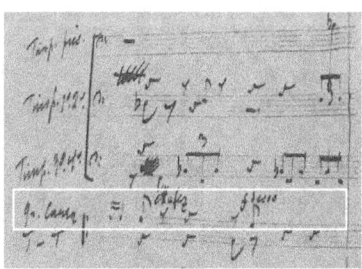

(Sketches, 1911-1913)

The timpani, bass drum, and tam-tam players, besides needing to be rhythmically precise (bass drum *secco* meaning dry), also need to muffle on the rests so that each instrument's entrance is clearly heard. The tam-tam must be able to speak quickly once again. It's interesting that the tam-tam notes come before the bass drum notes and not the other way around. The two timpanists should also be using the same mallets to ensure the triplets sound like one player. The tempo of the 5/4 section should also be anticipated from the previous 2/8 bar—the 8th equals the quarter of the 5/4 or the 16th equals the 8th note of the 5/4. One measure before reh. 181, some parts have the 2nd timpanist playing the low F and the 1st timpanist playing the high F. The 1st timpanist should play the low F and the 2nd timpanist, the high F since they're already playing those drums at those pitches previously. It should be noted that one bar before reh. 184, the F is missing from the Timpani II part in all scores and parts. Considering that it always appears before and after this phrase, it's a curious omission.

SACRIFICIAL DANCE (THE CHOSEN VICTIM)
REH. 186 TO THE END

The music from reh. 186 to the end poses one of the most difficult counting situations for the whole orchestra, including the conductor. It has been rebeamed, rebarred, and even the note values have been changed. Nonetheless, the bass drummer and timpanist should mark their parts in whatever way makes it as easy as possible to perform their parts. There will not be any looking at the conductor here.

The timpani part from reh. 189 to the end is the excerpt on every timpani audition and is one of the most famous timpani passages in the repertoire. Constant subdividing of 16th notes for both the bass drum and timpani is imperative. The timpanist should have the bass drum notes written in their part starting one m. after reh. 186 so that there's no hesitation with the first entrance. The problem is that while the bass drum is playing, the timpanist needs to tune an A and C. Since counting these meters at the same time while tuning two notes can be difficult, one option is to count how many notes the bass drum actually plays (six, the last being the only one *not* on a downbeat in current versions).

Around three or four bass drum notes in, the timpanist should be done tuning and back to looking at the music and counting. The bass drum and tuba's notes combined simulate what the timpanist will play in their entrance. The bass drum notes must answer the tuba and place their notes 100% perfectly. Think 2-3 subdivisions in the 5/16. Four m. before reh. 189, the last three notes fall in a way that subdividing quarter notes instead of 16ths can help, especially the last two notes:

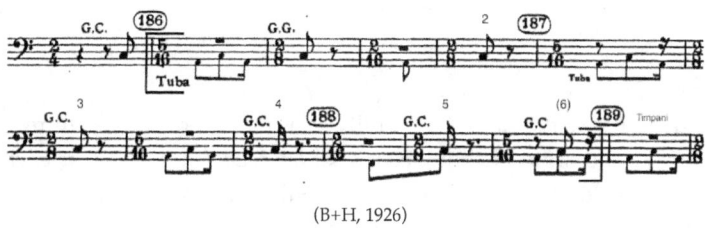

(B+H, 1926)

The timpanist must also be sure to not overplay. Make a difference with every note dynamic.

In the very first measure of reh. 189, there is an accent written on the third 16th note in most scores (original manuscript has no accent) but not on the subsequent 16th notes. This accent should be ignored:

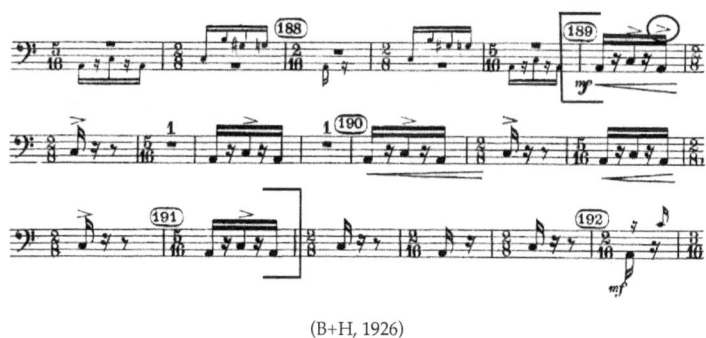

(B+H, 1926)

It will help to think of the phrases between reh. 189–191 subdivided as 2-3 and the rests as 3-2 for the 5/16 bars. The notes also need to have forward motion. The way to show that is to simply play the notes quite literally.

On each complete phrase between reh. 189–191, start *mezzo*

forte, then up a notch, down slightly on the 16th, but more than the first note, concluding with the biggest note on the next C:

(B+H, 1926)

Don't take the rests too literally and muffle on every 16th rest. Muffling before each downbeat C should be enough. After each crescendo to C, the next entrance should always start *mezzo forte* again, not where the crescendo left off. This dynamic contrast should be kept steadily till the *sforzando* in reh. 192, which should be bigger than any note in this section so far. The bass drum will assist with this, but can easily overplay. Doubling the timpani parts (a2) as discussed later will help. Then in the *mezzo forte*, *sforzando*, and *meno forte* notes, the *meno fortes* need to be slightly more than the *mezzo fortes*. Consult with the bass drummer and agree what dynamics will be played and where the *sforzandos* will be exactly. Here is the whole last unmarked page for reference:

Sacrificial Dance (The Chosen Victim) | 65

(B+H, 1926)

Even though the counting can be difficult, most of the timpani phrases follow similar patterns and have evenly distributed notes that can be counted much more easily. That being said, there are a few spots that need special attention:

- Two m. before reh. 193: there's a longer space between these notes than before, so don't be early one measure before reh. 193.
- Same as above, two m. before reh. 194.
- Two m. before reh. 196: same as above.
- Two m. before reh. 197: same as above.
- First two m. of reh. 197: there's an even longer gap of an extra 16th note between the first and second note. Count and don't be early on the second 16th.

Four m. before reh. 195 to the downbeat should be counted as five evenly spaced notes and played that way instead of trying to "fit" each one where written. This happens again four before reh. 198 and then the second bar of reh. 198 to the end. The second bar of reh. 198 starts the long crescendo to the final note. It can be more effective to come down in volume to make a more dramatic crescendo to reh. 201. To make the counting even easier for the timpanist, start counting how many times the A is played (ten times) starting the third m. of reh. 198:

(B+H, 1926)

It's important to note that starting at reh. 195, some timpani notes are notated a2. As seen in Berlioz's *Symphonie Fantastique*, when a2 is noted in the bass drum part, two bass drummers are required to play:

Sacrificial Dance (The Chosen Victim) | 67

In some cymbal parts, a2 distinguishes between suspended cymbal and crash cymbals (two cymbals). If Stravinsky meant two mallets, there usually is a stem up and stem down on the same note as Berlioz notated in the "March to the Scaffold":

Roman numerals are again sometimes notated—drums III and IV for the A and I and II for the C—but now a2 for each note. If we took this literally, the two low drums would be tuned to an A and the higher two drums to a C. Does Stravinsky really want the timpanist to sway back and forth everywhere a2 is notated? Also, the 2nd timpanist isn't instructed to have these pitched drums in their setup because their notes did not consist of anything below a D in the whole piece. We can deduce that Stravinsky simply wants these notes doubled and it's up to us how best to achieve that with the specific set up used. In later editions, it's more clear that it's left up to the players as how to execute these notes—each timpanist plays an A and a C—most likely from reh. 196 to the end. These examples might look different than what's in the parts (and not all a2 markings are clear which notes they should be over), so make sure both timpanists discuss which notes will be doubled:

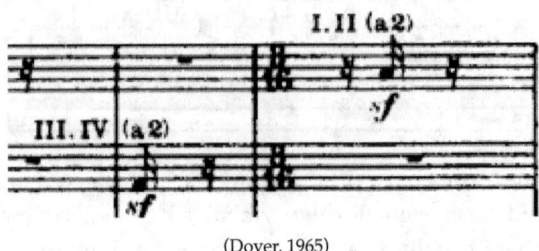

(Dover, 1965)

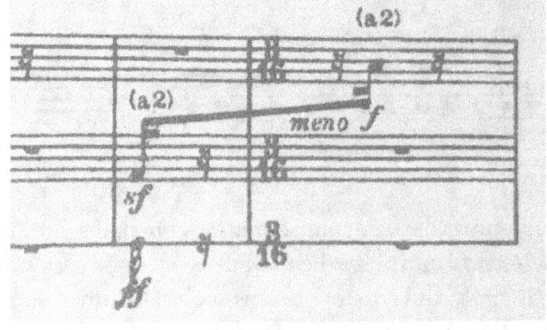

(Nieweg, 2000)

At reh. 195 and 196, the bass drum reinforces the *sforzando* notes between the timpanists with powerful blows. Similar to the 1st timpani part, the two bars at reh. 197 need to be counted carefully so as to not enter early on the 16th note in the 2/8 bar (in some editions of the score, this note doesn't even appear). The third m. of reh. 197 through 198 and third m. of reh. 198 through the end are all equally spaced notes as well. Maintaining a perfect unison rhythm and paced crescendo with the timpani is crucial.

Another never-ending curiosity is the myriad of changes from reh. 201 to the end. Although adding cymbal and güiro isn't as common, it's possible a conductor will ask for one of them. The 1921 score is the only one containing güiro (the cracking of the "Chosen One's" neck) and is still used today:

Sacrificial Dance (The Chosen Victim) | 69

(RMV, 1921)

(Cyr, Louis. "Writing The Rite Right" p.172)[10]

- If playing the güiro at the end, it is to be played as a scrape, not four individual 16th notes.
- Even though the notation and note placement of both bass drum and cymbal changes, it's assumed that examples 2–6 are cymbal notes (crashed or with stick on suspended) on the downbeat of reh. 201 (bass drum as well on example 5).

Sacrificial Dance (The Chosen Victim) | 71

- Second measure of reh. 201, suspended cymbal with stick; choke right away (*éttoufez*).
- Example 1 has a suspended cymbal scrape with the flutes and strings:

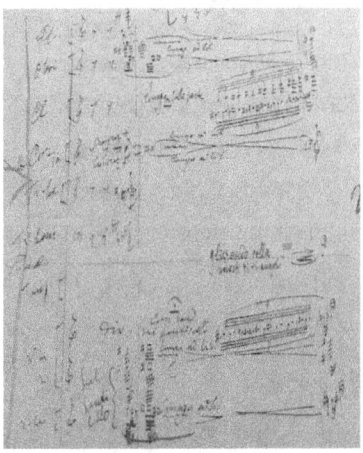

(Sketches, 1911-1913)

- Assuming the bass drum notes are all on the lower part of the staff, examples 2–7 all end with a crash cymbal and güiro (scrape before) on the final note.
- One of Bernstein's scores indicates "güiro (rasp)" before the last note, but many of his recordings have a ratchet instead. In percussionist Buster Bailey's part, it's noted "Play last beat on ratchet":

(New York Philharmonic Archives)[11]

The last chord of the piece contains possibly the final discrepancy for the timpani part. Depending on the score,

72 | THE RITE OF SPRING

Timpani II will have either a G-natural, G-sharp, or no note at all:

(RMV, 1921)

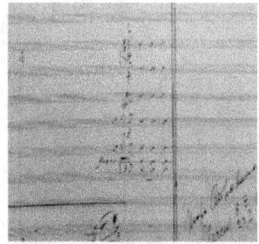

(Autograph facsimile, 2013)

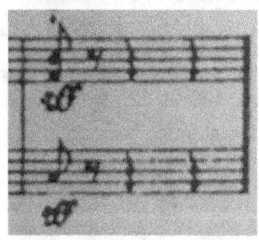

(B+H, 1943)

Sacrificial Dance (The Chosen Victim) | 73

(Dover, 1965)

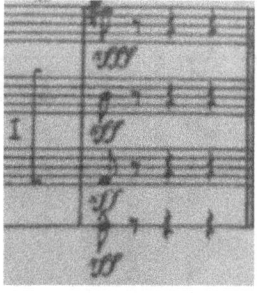

(Nieweg, 2000)

Considering the consistent G-sharps in the low strings and newer scores correcting what seems to be a blatant error in older scores, it makes sense to play a G-sharp. Stravinsky seems to want this note to stick out of the texture more than the other timpani and bass drum notes. He writes *sfff* compared to the other *sff* dynamics, maybe to make up for the fact that the other drums are a2.

The 1st timpanist has a double stop on A and D (in the 1926 parts, it's written "Timp II" on the A for some reason and 2nd timpanist playing the D). In some editions, the A and D are written for one player, but some have a2 over each note. If we follow our previous conclusion regarding the a2 marking, both A and D need to be doubled.

Depending on the setup, there are several options:

- 1st timpanist plays A and D. 2nd timpanist plays A and D. A third player plays the high G-sharp.
- 1st timpanist plays A and D. 2nd timpanist plays A, D, and high G-sharp (two mallets in one hand). This might not be ideal to get a precise attack, powerful enough sound, and to be able to muffle fast enough.
- 1st timpanist plays A and D. 2nd timpanist plays A *or* D only and the high G-sharp.

Perhaps the last mystery is the fact that the last chord in the basses spell, from low to high- D-E-A-D!

(B+H, 1926)

AFTERWORD

When performance time comes, there's always extra adrenaline and anxiety. Stravinsky's own philosophy might help. When rehearsing the dance passages (basses, timpani, and tutti orchestra), he recommended the timpanists and bassists think of themselves as a pianist's left hand and the tutti orchestra as the pianist's right hand. This seemed to improve the precision and rhythmic feel, especially in the "Sacrificial Dance."

While *The Rite* may not be as challenging as it was 100 years ago, it's always a thrill. If a percussionist is lucky enough to get the chance, extra time and effort should be put into studying the part. Listen to as many recordings as possible, study the score, practice conducting the time changes, master your part, and continue to reference this guide. It will all be worth it in the end!

ENDNOTES

[1] Nadia Boulanger, *Once at a Border: Aspects of Stravinsky*, DVD, Tony Palmer, director (Long Branch, NJ: Kultur International Films, 1986).

[2] Pieter C. Van den Toorn, *Stravinsky and The Rite of Spring* (Oxford: Oxford University Press, 1987), 39.

[3] Robert Craft, "The Performance of the 'Rite of Spring,'" in *The Rite of Spring, Sketches 1911-1913: Facsimile Reproductions from the Autographs* (London: Boosey & Hawkes, 1969), 46.

[4] Ibid.

[5] Ibid.

[6] Ibid.

[7] Ibid, 47.

[8] Ibid.

[9] Charles L. White, *Tympani Instructions for Playing Igor Stravinsky's "Sacre du printemps"* (Los Angeles: Charles L. White, 1965), 30.

[10] Louis Cyr, "Writing *The Rite* Right," in *Confronting Stravinsky: Man, Musician and Modernist*, edited by Jann Pasler (Berkeley: University of California Press, 1986), 172.

[11] Stravinsky, *The Rite of Spring*. Performance parts in the New York Philharmonic Leon Levy Digital Archives, set 31, set A, percussion part. Available online at https://archives.nyphil.org/index.php/artifact/060b3669-cedd-4c30-8ed7-2d2c2db0a94a-0.1.

BIBLIOGRAPHY
(Arranged chronologically by creation/publication)

Stravinsky, Igor. *The Rite of Spring, Sketches 1911–1913: Facsimile Reproductions from the Autographs*. London: Boosey & Hawkes, 1969

———. *Le Sacre du printemps: Facsimile of the Autograph Full Score*. Edited by Ulrich Mosch. Centenary Edition, volume 1. Berlin: Paul Sacher Foundation; London: Boosey & Hawkes, 2013.

———. *Le Sacre du printemps*. Berlin: Russischer Musik-Verlag; Édition Russe de Musique, 1921

———. *Le Sacre du printemps*. Berlin: Russischer Musik-Verlag; Edition Russe de Musique, [1921, 1926]. Edition no. R.M.V. 198. [Orchestral parts].

———. *Le Sacre du Printemps: Danse Sacrale*. Revised version, 1943. New York: Associated Music Publishers, 1945.

———. *Le Sacre du printemps*. [Paris]: Edition Russe de Musique, 1921; New York: Boosey & Hawkes, 1947, [1967]. Edition no. 16603. [Orchestral parts]

———. The Rite of Spring. Moscow: Izdatel'stvo "Muzyka" [Russian State Music Publishing House], 1965. Reprint: Mineola, NY: Dover Publications, 1989 [full score], 2000 [study score].

———. *The Rite of Spring*. Edited by Clinton F. Nieweg. Boca Raton, FL: Edwin F. Kalmus, 2000.

ABOUT THE AUTHOR

A native of Boston, Massachusetts, percussionist Chris DeChiara received his education from New England Conservatory (MM) with Academic Honors and Distinction in Performance and from the University of Massachusetts at Lowell (BM), graduating cum laude. He has performed with the Boston Ballet, Boston Lyric Opera, Boston Philharmonic, Rhode Island Symphony, Kennedy Center Opera Orchestra, Boston Modern Orchestra Project, Concert Artists of Baltimore, Harrisburg Symphony, and National Philharmonic. He has participated in the Rome Festival Orchestra, Aspen Music Festival, Spoleto, Schleswig-Holstein, and was principal percussionist of the World Philharmonic concert in Bonn, Germany, 1999. Published articles appear in issues of *Modern Drummer* magazine.

Chris is currently a member and soloist with the United States Navy Band in Washington DC, drummer of the local cover band, Dr.FU and Iron Maiden tribute Eyes of the Nile, lead singer of Beatles acoustic group Nowhere Men, principal timpanist with the conductorless chamber group, ARS Nova Ensemble, and principal timpanist with Pro Arte Chamber Orchestra of Washington. He conveys his passion for the arts by mentoring the next generation of musicians, teaching masterclasses, clinics, private lessons, percussion ensembles, drumlines, and coaching orchestral and concert band percussion sections in the DC metropolitan region.

Chris resides in Burke, VA, maintaining a home studio where he teaches, produces drum and percussion videos, and records drum and percussion tracks for artists of all genres. More information is available at www.chrisdechiara.com.

www.ingramcontent.com/pod-product-compliance
Lightning Source LLC
Chambersburg PA
CBHW071409290426
44108CB00014B/1744